THE BOOK

MARY RUEFLE

The Book

WAVE BOOKS

SEATTLE & NEW YORK

Published by Wave Books

www.wavepoetry.com

Copyright © 2023 by Mary Ruefle

All rights reserved

Wave Books titles are distributed to the trade by

Consortium Book Sales and Distribution

Phone: 800-283-3572 / SAN 631-760X

Library of Congress Cataloging-in-Publication Data

Names: Ruefle, Mary, 1952– author.

Title: The book / Mary Ruefle.

Description: First edition. I Seattle : Wave Books, [2023]

Identifiers: LCCN 2023009940 I ISBN 9781950268849 (hardcover)

Subjects: LCGFT: Prose poems.

Classification: LCC PS3568.U36 B66 2023 I DDC 811/.54–dc23/eng/20230301

LC record available at https://lccn.loc.gov/2023009940

Designed by Crisis

Printed in the United States of America

9 8 7 6 5 4 3 2 1

First Edition

Wave Books 110

DEAR FRIENDS, THIS IS FOR YOU

Contents

They're gone now. It makes me sad to think about it.
Feeling old, for no reason at all
I picked a bit of mint from the ditch.

FRANCIS JAMMES

The Book

UNTITLED

About this time I began to suspect I was never named; people called me Mary because it was convenient, or because they had heard others call me Mary, I was in the beginning named after someone else who was named Mary but I was neither this person nor the one they called Mary after her, I was nameless, and in this state I perpetually wandered among fruit and flowers and foliage, among vines and overhanging rock and untamed animals, none of whom I could name, none of whom knew my name, nor, if they did, could they speak it. I read once that the Amazon was called the Green Hell, and if that is a name, I take it, if only as a substitute for my unknown name, which not even my parents knew when they named me Mary, after a woman who scrubbed her kitchen floor on her hands and knees, once a week, with a stiff brush. She was kind to me and I loved her, and since her death I have dreamt of her many times, either searching for her or speaking to her, but never once in my dreams have I called her Mary, which, I suspect, is not her name, or if it once was, is no longer.

THE PHOTOGRAPH

I have a photograph that was taken more than a hundred years ago. I am related to its subject but don't know who she is, I don't know whether I am related to her through my mother or through my father, they hadn't been born when the photograph was taken and they are dead now. I don't know where the picture was taken except on the porch steps of an old wooden house, and I stare at her who is sitting on the steps, about thirty with dark hair, looking like no one I know, almost expressionless before the camera, I stare at her and it *looks* like she is looking at me but I know she hasn't a clue that she is looking at me, she looks right through me, she is looking at her photographer, and I think I see a strand of hair about to fall over one eye, maybe she is thinking about that, I don't know, but there is a deep and abiding bond between us, I feel it, even if she doesn't know my mother's name or my father's name, whether they lived past infancy or at all. We are both alive, she in the picture and I with the picture in my hands, and we both know nothing of the other—perhaps that is the bond between us, though she is certainly not thinking about the future in which *I* am the unknown relative. And then I realize she *is* thinking about the future, she is *waiting* for the future, she is waiting for the small unmistakable sound of the shutter, the click of the camera signifying that something is over, and I do not think we can be any more specific than that, so I blink and let that be the sign between us.

PIXIE

It was the day of my first haircut, which was the day of my last haircut, it was the day of my first trip to the hairdresser, which was the day of my last, it was what I might now call the Day of the Great Shorning, for I was led like a lamb by my mother through the door of the glass-fronted shop, the door had curly black lettering painted right on the glass (I couldn't read, I was wearing a dress) and then we were in a room full of women, I called them ladies then, they were all talking at once (how did they find so many things to do with their mouths?) but my mother was not talking, she was whispering the way she whispered on Christmas Eve or the morning of my birthday, and I felt a great surprise was in store for me, or so it seemed when I was caped like a princess and set on a throne, a big padded chair, the chair itself was a surprise for it turned like a planet, and as if it were night I was turned away from the light, I was no longer facing the mirror, and though my back was to the light there were wonderful things to look at, potions were lined up on shelves, bottles full of colored water, one had a comb suspended in it like a shark in the aquarium, perhaps I would be able to take it home, it would look nice in my room, I was so intent on taking it home (I would have to buy fish food) I didn't hear the scissors, I didn't hear my own hair falling from off my head and onto the floor, but when I looked down I could see the lifeless piles of it scattered like chicken feed (would I be sent to a farm?) and then the planet spun round again and I was looking in the mirror at the face of a stranger, a hairless pixie with the ears of an elf, and she so scared me (I had heard you could be frightened to *death*) I leapt out of my throne like a dolphin (my aunt and uncle lived near the ocean, I could go to them) and ran through the door with the curly black lettering (it looked like seaweed to me now), I was through the door and down the street when I collided with my mother, it was brutal, but even in those moments my hair was starting to grow back (*it would grow back in time* was what my mother said, and so it did), it grew through the years until I could toss it, now it is like a bridal train when I walk, it wraps me like an octopus when I bathe, but the child who wanted to feed a comb is unrecognizable to me, and belongs to another century.

THE WRAPPED BOOK

A long, long time ago I lived briefly in Switzerland, in an Alpine village with a single bookstore, one which sold books in many languages, including English, and whenever they sold a book they would wrap it in plain blue paper and tie it with string, like a present. I had never seen such a custom and loved it. I decided to always keep a book wrapped in plain blue paper on my shelves, some book I knew I would love, some book whose title and author I would have forgotten by the time I unwrapped it. And so I did, for years, but more often than not by the time I unwrapped the book it was a book I had already read, or a book that I did not exactly love. Still, it was of great solace to me to have a wrapped book on my shelves. I have such a book now and am afraid to open it, it is not in plain blue paper but in shiny paper, a shiny photograph of some rocky island in some blue sea. A magazine page? It has sat among my books for many years, how many I cannot say. I have no idea what book is inside. I will open it one day but not today. I want to be surprised, I want the book to delight me, I want it to be the most perfect book in the world, but I am afraid of being disappointed. I know when I wrapped the book it seemed perfect to me, but times have changed and I have changed and all my hopes have been redirected. It seems I believe in a bygone world though I no longer live there. Will I continue to read about all that is dusty? I am not brave enough to open the book wrapped in an island in the middle of a sea I cannot name. *Strait Is the Gate* is the name of the book I bought in the Alpine village, and took home and ripped open.

NETTLES

If everyone were a storyteller, the infrastructure of the village would collapse. With more than one teller—with so many—contention and conflict would ensue. The one true storyteller—who can say which one?—would be compelled to retire to a cave and sit silent for ten years, eating nothing but nettles and drinking the tea that can be made from them. When he (she? they?) came out, the village would be going about its daily business, digging tubers, nursing babies, drying meat, all of which had already been put into a story by everyone else, so that no story would be left to tell, except the story of the one true storyteller, how he had lived in a cave for ten years, nettled by his own silence, and had at last emerged and found no one willing to listen.

THE BARK

I took my dog to the lake, he stood at the water's edge and barked, the echo of his bark came back and he barked at it, again and again he barked at his own echo, thinking there was another dog on the other side of the lake. *Welcome to poetry*, I said.

NOPE

I was in a big city and visited its famous independent bookstore. It was huge, I had trouble finding the poetry and had to ask for help. I sat myself down on the floor in front of all the poetry and looked over the titles. There were so many! I found poets I loved, poets who were my friends, poets I had known who were now dead, poets I had met once and never seen again (but always remembered), poets I had never heard of, all manner of poets, but all these books just made me sad in the end—I knew nobody read them. *I* read them, but when I did I just started writing poems myself, creating an endless loop that depressed me. Just then a teenaged boy passed by with his mother, they paused in front of the poetry section and the boy said "Look! I found the poetry, dad is always telling me to look for the poetry, to find the poetry—well, here it is, I've found it!" He was making a joke at his father's expense, but his mother seemed moved, for she said "Would you like to buy a book of poetry?" and the boy said "Nope!" and ambled away. A wave of ridiculous but deep happiness swept over me, suddenly I was feeling so happy I got up and left the store without buying a single book.

WE NEED TO TALK

ABOUT ICE CREAM

Choose five artists you deeply admire for being extraordinary and make a documentary film in which each one is shown, for ten minutes, in violent argument with their spouse or partner, revealing the artist's mean, low, reprehensible side.

THE CANDY

I was not even sure I wanted to see him once more before he died, and if I did it seemed a kind of madness, he meant nothing to me now, less than nothing, but the cold mountainous landscape in which we met, and in which I knew he still lived, had haunted me for half of a century. When I lie sleepless at night, I count snowflakes the way some people count sheep, I have a friend who counts sheep and she told me the sheep are really little lambs jumping over a low wooden fence, but this, I think, is no different than counting horses or dogs. The snow I see falls, it cannot be mistaken for anything other than large flat white crystals, no two alike, and I count them horizontally, on a plane of sorts, for they are falling side by side through the air, slowly and continuously, accumulating on the ground. We, he and I, walked through such snow on the evening we met, and when we reached my door (he was walking me home after an evening spent in the company of a great many others) we began to retrace our steps through the snow, walking back to the place we had started from, we did this without a word between us, it was an unspoken agreement that we did not want the walk to come to an end and therefore repeated it, I cannot say how many repetitions we made of our walk, but a ten-minute walk lasted more than an hour. Neither of us spoke as we walked, not a word passed between us, but one can listen to falling snow, anyone who does not believe this has never walked silently through the veil of it, if rain can speak why not snow, the way a wet, sobbing heart can still be heard beating when it is cold and withdrawn. It snowed for five days. The house I lived in was buried in snow and time became fainter and fainter until neither of us knew what day it was and had to ask the other *what day is it? is it Friday or Saturday? was it Sunday or Monday?* We could not remember and we always disagreed, about that and a great many other things, as it happened. It was cold, it was messy, I didn't like it (later I moved to the desert), once my parents had taken me as a girl to the German Alps, it was a skiing holiday, and while my parents skied, for they were athletic and to their great disappointment I was not, I joined a bus tour with the elderly (elderly to me then, I am of their age now), we crossed into Austria to visit the famous castle of mad King Ludwig (we were told the Disneyland castle was based on its very pinnacles) but the castle bored me, all I remember is that when the king disagreed with a dinner guest, he opened a trapdoor beneath the table and his guest fell a long way into a cold stone dungeon; that was one day, it snowed that day and all of the other days, days I spent sitting in our rented chalet reading a novel while eating chocolates from a box, I picked one up and ate it without even bothering to look at it, each piece was nestled in an indentation, the indentations were on a single sheet of molded brown plastic, and when the chocolates were gone I turned the molding upside down and it looked like the little village of houses we were staying in—I did like the snow on the roofs of the houses, and the snow on the mountaintop was magnificent, even if the skiers were repeatedly streaking down it in a kind of madness, like tears, or what struck me as tears when seen from below, or above, or standing a little ways off to the side, I mean the madness, the past, the fantasy, the trapdoor, whatever leads to the future.

HOUSE HUNTING

When we lived in the blue house we were happy. But it didn't have a porch or a fireplace, and we knew these things would make us happier. That was when we bought the yellow house with a porch and a fireplace, and we were happy in the summer sitting on our porch, and happy in the winter sitting in front of the fire, but we weren't happy in the kitchen or the bedroom or the living room of that yellow house, fall and spring were especially hard, when it was too cold to use the porch and too warm to build a fire. That was when we bought the white house, where we were happy in the kitchen and in the bedroom and in the living room, and we had a porch and a fireplace— having once had them we would never give them up. The porch was smaller than our first porch but we didn't mind a bit. The fireplace was larger, though, and even if the fire was roaring all the heat in the house went straight up the chimney and we began to actually shiver. We were so cold we put on our coats and went for a drive, we drove past the blue house and looked at it with nostalgia, we drove past the yellow house and got a lump in our throats, but not so big we couldn't swallow it. On our way home we passed a red house with no one in it, there was no For Sale sign but we decided to have a look anyway, we walked around the red house and peeked in all the windows, and there were a great many of them. So much light and privacy! The house was set back from the road and had an enormous yard behind it, it seemed to go on forever and then continue into the woods that bordered on a state park that bordered on a national one. With so much privacy we wouldn't need a porch, and with so much light we wouldn't need a fire. But without a For Sale sign, who should we call? We decided to ask around, so we drove to the nearest house and knocked on the door. Is the house next door for sale? we asked. The red house? they said. It's been like that for years. But who lives there? we said. No one, they said, but the deer like it so much they come at every dusk to graze. Who owns it? we asked. Why, we do, they said, it's ours to look at, we bought it so we could see the deer, we can sit out in the evenings and watch them grazing. Will you sell it? we asked. If we lived there you could still see the deer. I doubt it, they said. The deer like their privacy, they aren't happy when people are around. We pleaded, but those crummy happy people wouldn't budge. So we said goodbye to the happy deer, who, it turns out, were an endangered breed of tiny reindeer with spots and delicate antlers.

A LESSON IN HISTORY

My student hated history. History is stupid, he said. Stuff that's already happened is boring. Maybe a history of parties might be slightly interesting, like on one page or something, but there's no history of parties because you go to a party to forget history—that's the point. You party. Only an idiot doesn't get it. If you remember anything, it wasn't a party. Jesus. Ok, take him. The only thing you need to know about Jesus is that he's famous for throwing a dinner party. Take the Greek tragedies. The famous plays and stuff. People who have read them are so proud of it, but wasn't it pride that did old man Eddie in? What a pussy. Cultured people are so blind they can't see what makes them civilized: it's pride. It's insane. They might as well eat powdered glass. We do that at parties sometimes.

MY LIFE AS A SCHOLAR

My friend the metalsmith told me that the first piece of jewelry she learned to make as an apprentice was a fibula, the earliest form of a pin, used by the ancient Greeks and Romans to fasten their togas. It is used today on Scottish kilts, in miniature we call it a safety pin, and until the advent of disposable diapers it was the ubiquitous diaper pin. I was teaching undergraduates at the time, and immediately signed up to teach the Greek tragedies—Oedipus, upon learning that he had gone to bed with his mother, stabbed out his eyes with a diaper pin!

THE CASHEW

Throughout the play, a man or woman is sleeping on a divan set to the side of the stage (where it will not interfere with the comings and goings of the actors). Ideally, the sleeper is curled in the shape of a cashew. At no particular moment, but once during each act, the sleeper half-rises and, as if from a window of lucidity, says, "I'm trying to stay calm." This "character," whoever he is (a stranger thrust into the circumstances unfolding around him? the playwright? Shakespeare? Brecht?) then resumes his peaceful sleep.

These stage directions may be introduced into any play, but if they are introduced into all plays, is it certain or doubtful that the course of theater has been changed?

Keep your essay to a minimum of five hundred words.

MY MEMORY OF A STORY BY LYDIA DAVIS I READ YEARS AGO AND *NEVER FORGOT*

A Russian, Wassilly, is mysteriously escorted to a snowbound village in the Eastern wilds. On the way there, bells ring in the icy air. A sleigh? In the village, which is practically empty, strangers act in strange and unsettling ways. Dogs begin to bark. Faces peer out of the windows. Dogs continue to bark. As the story ends, the thin cold air is filled with faint and faraway barks . . .

THE STAGEHAND

My job is to remove the shoes from the stage floor at the end of the
first act, those belonging to the Countess, sweet low-heeled slippers
of rose-colored satin with a square marcasite buckle. And again at
the end of the third act, only this time there are three pairs, those
of the dead Countess and her lover, and those of the witless Count
who has murdered them before killing himself. I remove the shoes
at the end so none of the actors will trip over them when they take
their curtain call, which is when I stand in the wings and think *if it*
weren't for me there would be a disaster.

THE TREES

It will soon be noon. You may put on your hat, and we will go out. It is a hot day, so we will sit in the cool shade of the trees. We can see the flowers in bloom and hear the birds sing. When it is cool we will go back to the house. We have cut down those trees that were near, for they made a dark shade, and there was a deep gloom in my room.

WHAT HAPPENS WHEN YOU DIE

As it happens, I travel a lot, therefore I am in a good position to know what happens when you die. When you die, a plane takes off, another plane lands, people of all ages travel rapidly forward on the moving sidewalk between terminals. A traveler between connections stops at a kiosk and buys a damp turkey sandwich, another one buys a fruit smoothie and still another, weary but with more time, stops for a beer at the airport bar. A man in the gift shop buys a box of molasses candy for his wife, while a woman he thinks attractive picks up a plastic airplane for her son. A flight attendant rolls her bag effortlessly through security. An airline employee at gate 32 deals with an irate passenger, who will afterwards feel guilty for ruining her day. There is a small crisis in the bathroom, swiftly attended to. The electric cart moving between gates carries a passenger who can no longer walk, and barely misses running into one who can. A plane is late. Another one is early. All this happens when you die, and if you don't believe me you are alone, and stranded beyond help.

THE CLOUD BEATERS

It was a winter's noon, ice-cold and sunny, when I saw in a single bare tree a hundred or more birds flitting in and out of the branches, lunching on withered berries. The sun hit the breasts of the birds and they all shone like hammered gold. I described this event to my friend and she asked what kind of birds they were. But I could not remember the name of the birds, the word had receded to a space in my mind I could not reach. "Cloud Beaters" came out of my mouth —where that came from I'll never know, it may be it came from the same place the forgotten word lived. "Oh, cedar waxwings!" she cried. I had struggled, I had tried, I had come as close as I could, I didn't have the words, but she knew what I meant.

THE TRANSLATOR

Two insects exchanged information in the middle of the night. Perhaps they were frogs, I can't say, but the shrilling carried far; I woke in my bed and did not turn on the light, four times the information was relayed and came back verbatim, or maybe countered with questions, *did I hear you correctly? are you absolutely certain? could you repeat it?* And then they quit. A phone call after midnight means accident or death (I have received both) and though I know it may have been a creaturely announcement of love and ripeness (those too) it sounded like dire info to my ear. I lay there, wondering. Was it something that I, too, would like to know or needed unbeknownst to know, something that would affect me personally, if only I knew? What *were* they saying, out there in the night? To pay such close attention, to hear with every fiber of my being, and remain completely ignorant.

GOLDEN CRUMBS

Ever, when the two ladies were having a quiet cup of tea in the great, big, uncomfortable drawing-room on the first floor, with its conventional wilderness of chairs and silly little tables laden with uninteresting bric-a-brac, they heard the front doorbell ring, and began to speculate who the visitor might be. Week after week, on a Tuesday a little after four, the bell rang once and once only, there was silence thereafter, and as the years passed the two ladies came to regard this event as the great mystery of their lives.

LOVE STORY

The one winter I spent by water I would walk out on the ice every evening at dusk after the ice fishermen had abandoned their shanty. I would peer into the window of stapled plastic and watch the stick of frozen butter as it lay there on a plywood counter. I don't know what the butter was for. I knew they built fires on the ice for warmth and drank out of bottles for warmth, but butter in the shanty? I never saw them actually cook, they would take the fish home, home not being the shanty, the shanty being a temporary winter dwelling where they could store their gear and stuff. The sun would set, throwing a glare on the ice, and sometimes I saw through the window that it cast a glare on that stick of butter. I went back every day to check on the butter. It was never unwrapped, it was never cut. And then spring came, overnight the shanty sank on a doily of slush and the butter went with it. I never asked, I never found out, but as the days grew warmer, warm enough to melt butter over an afternoon, I often thought to myself that it was the perfect love story, and I was glad the butter had disappeared overnight and not stuck around to melt.

THE WIND

I once received a two-page letter—typed, single-spaced—with nothing in it. The individual words had meaning, as all words do, but when you set the meanings side by side they became meaningless. I must have read that letter three or four times before I realized the only thing I actually knew was that I felt empty and sad and the world felt drained of beauty on account of that letter with nothing in it. As I ripped the letter up—I had been reading it at a picnic table—a sudden gust of wind blew the many fragments of paper into a nearby bush. It was suddenly very interesting—the bush not the letter—so I photographed it, then forgot about it. Weeks later I had the film developed and there was the letter in many pieces, each of which had snagged somewhere on the bush. I could still read some of the words. And that photo had meaning, looking at it I saw at once it had meaning, while the letter had had none. I think this has something to do with art.

THE COLOR

I was at my desk pretending to be writing. Actually I *really was* writ-
ing, but while writing I was really thinking about things that had noth-
ing to do with what I was writing—and there were quite a few of
them—and even now I must stop and think about that strange phrase
quite a few, for how can there be *quite a few*, if there are few there
are few, but wouldn't *quite a few* be a lot, quite a lot as a matter of
fact? Now I am done thinking about that, but this morning, while pre-
tending to write, I was thinking that I had made a terrible mistake in
choosing the fabric of my new curtains, no, not the fabric but the
color of the fabric (to be exact) (and one must strive for something),
the color was too light, it needed to be ten shades darker, not a light
wheat-colored straw but a dark golden straw, clearly I had made a
terrible mistake and was now deeply in debt to my better judgment,
such as it is (there are days my better judgment and I are not even
on speaking terms), and there I sat, on and on I sat, pretending to
write but secretly obsessed with what I had done, what I had done
of my own free will, such as it is. I had irreversibly chosen, out of all
the colors in the world, *the wrong one*. A titanic mistake! And as I sat
there, many past instances of identical horror came back to me, like
ghosts who were hungry and came home to eat everything they

could lay their hands on, which was quite a lot. How could I pretend to be writing when the room was full of ghosts, when all my mistakes were hovering over me, demanding my attention, gobbling, always gobbling something? I could pretend to pretend—the thought occurred to me—it had worked in the past—but the ghosts wouldn't fall for it, I knew that, they would be thinking *there she is, pretending to be writing, her old ploy, what a scam.* And so I tricked them, I no longer pretended to be writing, I just stopped, I stopped suddenly and cleanly, throwing them a loop I hoped would take them out the window.

THE PERK

He was just a clown. Of medium height, a little fat, a little clumsy. I don't remember his name but I remember the day I called the pizza parlor and asked if they could arrange a child's birthday party for my husband, who was turning fifty. My husband was boyish, had a terrific sense of humor and loved pizza, so my bright idea was a child's party with balloons and paper hats and a clown. Plus each guest got to go into the kitchen and make their own pizza. They did all that stuff for children. The manager of the pizza parlor told me it wasn't possible, they wouldn't do it for an adult, it was too weird. I was so disappointed I asked if I might leave my name and number in case he changed his mind. Think it over, I said. I don't think he wanted to think it over, but not wanting to be impolite he agreed to take my name and number. When I gave him my name there was a pause before he said Mary Ruefle, the poet? I was completely taken aback, as far as I knew I wasn't known to anyone, except maybe four people in another state. That's me, I said. The manager explained that he had an MFA, he had read my work and enjoyed it, and he'd be happy to let me throw a kid's party for my husband in his pizza parlor. Again I was taken aback, because there were no known perks to being a poet, and here was a pizza joint rolling out the red carpet.

So I threw my husband the party. I thought our clown would be wearing a ruffled, polka-dotted jumpsuit but he was in a plain shirt and tie with a plastic clown mask over his face. He did a few magic tricks and twisted long balloons into dachshunds—I remember that because it seemed to me an amazing skill. One of the things the clown always did was to read a fairy tale to the kids, and for us he chose Hans Christian Andersen's "The Little Match Girl," where a poor little barefoot girl is wandering the streets on a bitterly cold and snowy night, trying to sell matches. If she goes home her father will beat her, for she hadn't sold a single match. To warm herself she strikes one match after another, and has a series of beautiful fantasies. In the morning she's found dead, frozen to death on the street. It was very strange, no one knew what to say, but we managed to have fun when we were in the kitchen making our own pizzas, and laughed about "The Little Match Girl" while throwing disks of pepperoni in the air, pretending they were matches. A few weeks later my husband, who was also a doctor, was called to the fourth floor of the hospital, the psych ward. As he walked down the hall to see a patient who had some object stuck up his nose, he saw the clown in a hospital gown shuffling towards him. Hello birthday boy, the clown said, and feebly waved. My husband asked him what he was doing there, on the psych ward; the clown said he had lost his job as a clown and had tried to kill himself. I am very sorry, my husband said, you were such a good clown. My husband came home that night and relayed the conversation. Neither of us could quite believe it, it was so sad. We lived out in the country on a dirt road and our closest neighbor, whom we didn't know, was six acres away. One day I walked past our neighbor's house and there was a trailer next to the house, a trailer with an open end facing the road. There was the clown, sitting at a little table inside, with a cot beside the table and something tacked on the wall. He looked up and saw me, our eyes met, and his face seemed to me to light up, just a glimmer, and then he waved at me, a feeble wave but still a wave. For a couple of days we waved at each other whenever I walked by, and one day the trailer was gone and I never saw him again, so I don't know how the story ends. Or where he is, or even if he's living. But we did return to the pizza parlor—the manager always came personally to "the poet's table"—and we asked why the clown had lost his job, and were told parents complained that all his stories were grim, and terrorized the children. And then we ordered a 16″ white pizza with spinach, artichokes, and garlic.

THE HEART, WHAT IS IT?

I was tired of writing my name and address on the corner of envelopes so I decided to have an inkstamp made. Standing in the store I realized that such stamps accommodate three lines. Three lines! That was the number of lines in a common haiku, so I immediately decided to have a haiku stamp made instead. But standing there I could not remember a single haiku by my favorite haiku master, Issa, so I gave them one I could remember, by Ikkyū, a fifteenth-century Zen monk and poet who was born and died in Kyoto.

> The heart, what is it,
> is it the sound of the pinetrees
> blowing in the painting?

When I went back to pick up the completed stamp, I was overcome with the feeling I had gotten it wrong, that I had misremembered the haiku; I could not shake this feeling so I called my friend Elena, a poet and translator, who had first introduced me to this haiku, which was her favorite. She said I had indeed gotten it wrong, Ikkyū's haiku was

> The heart, what is it,
>
> is it the sound of the pinetrees
>
> there in the painting?

I told her about the stamp and the word *blowing*, which suddenly I liked; she said that *there* was better because it left so much more to the imagination of the reader.

My argument in favor of *blowing* was that it didn't make much of a difference since the central—most important—words in the haiku came at the end—*in the painting*. Those words blew everything out of the water, they contradicted the idea of any sound whatsoever. The poem's power came from those three last words.

I called my friend Jody, a poet and translator, and asked her which version she preferred. She said *blowing* because it was more specific and an active verb. When someone agrees with you, it feels very good.

Then I asked Michael, my husband and a poet, and he did not hesitate to say he preferred *there*, because *there* suggested that the trees had a more dimensional life, that *blowing* was "too typical for trees."

Then I asked Jody to ask David, her husband, a poet and translator and Zen practitioner, to break the tie by saying which version he preferred. David said he didn't like either version because he didn't like the haiku to begin with—it was full of too many words and "not enough emptiness."

My opinion was that if someone wanted fewer and fewer words and more and more emptiness they shouldn't bother with poetry at all, they should neither read it nor write it but simply live their lives, walking through the city or the forest without a thought to language. I knew in my heart that the outer world was without written language and that pages of writing were ultimately meaningless, I knew all that, but I also knew that humans are peculiar and often lead long lives and try to do things that make them happy, and that writing was one of those ten thousand things.

Then Jody called me back and said she changed her mind, she definitely preferred the version with *there* in it, but that she would change the punctuation to

> The heart, what is it,
> is it the sound of the pinetrees
> there—in the painting?

But I still preferred *blowing* to *there*—I could see the trees bending in the wind and then WHAM I saw the painting, without movement, without sound, and thus was left at a standstill. After heart-movement heart-stillness, that seemed accurate to me. None of us knew

Japanese, and I have no idea how many different English translations have been made of the original, but I think Ikkyū could care less about the fate of his poem.

So there it is: Elena, Jody, and Michael prefer *there*, David doesn't like the haiku to begin with, and Ikkyū has no opinion.

I like *blowing* and I will not bend.

As usual, I have given you a piece of my heart.

I DREAM OF JUNG

A friend who was studying Buddhism made a pilgrimage to Tibet. She brought back a gift for me, two oblong pieces of metal, each slightly larger than a postage stamp, and told me she had bought them at a bazaar of sorts, old things sold on the street. They were a bright gold color, though I think made of copper or more probably an odd admixture of metals. Each one was embossed with what looked like flying scarves or banners and a round drumlike object that might have been a prayer wheel. Another friend of mine is a metalsmith, a jeweler, and I had her convert the two pieces into a pair of dangling earrings. Sometime later I had the dream: I was invited to Carl Jung's house for dinner, it was a party of around twelve people, and I wore the earrings; several of the guests admired them, and Jung himself came over to take a look. When he saw them he was aghast, horrified, furious, and he began to shout at me, saying it was sacrilege to turn such sacred objects into jewelry, into decorative trinkets. He was so upset he asked me to leave, and I was so deeply ashamed I did leave, but first I used Jung's bathroom and while raising the lid of his toilet I noticed it had been made out of an ancient African mask or shield—he had converted an oval totem into a lid for his john! Now it was my turn to be furious—I was furious at his hypocrisy, but also relieved and amused; I left Jung's house feeling we were comrades after all—brothers in hypocrisy, twin fools, the King & Queen of Cluelessness.

LUCKY DRAGON

God walked into the Lucky Dragon and, in a tired, half-dead voice, ordered a Shanghai spring roll, wonton soup, steamed dumplings, chicken fried rice, egg foo young, moo shu pork, sweet and sour shrimp, and General Tso's chicken. He loved everything, he ate everything, but the twelve fortune cookies that came after he did not care for, so he folded them carefully into the dough of a dozen unborn children, hoping for the best. While the staff remained watching from the kitchen door, God walked out slowly, absolutely full, unable to fly.

MY DYING FRIEND

I was visiting a dying friend in the hospital and passed by a room full of babies who had not yet been given names. They were all lined up in a row, like science projects. Those with names had won a bracelet and been taken away. But those who remained were quite interesting, judging by the sadness already evident in their features. What do I call thee, little lamb lying here on a bed of cotton? I stopped someone in a uniform who was familiar with them. "Come back tomorrow," she said, "they will all be gone."

DEAR FRIENDS

I have had friends, and have them now, but never once did I believe that in my lifetime the word *friend* would have a new, different, other meaning. I knew language evolved and changed over time, I knew there were new words every year to accommodate its growth and that some words changed meaning; but *love, death, flower, fire? Friend?* Then one day I picked up a magazine and read an interview with the COO (chief operating officer) of Facebook, perhaps she still is, I don't know, but she was asked how many friends she had and she said, "Over three thousand. I don't know all of them but I have met them in one shape or form." I would rather be antiquated—I would rather die—than make a statement like that. I *know* my friends, I know the sound of their voices, their speech patterns, their inflections, their hand and body gestures, the wet of their eyes, what makes them laugh, what makes them cry, how their nose was broken and how they became beautiful after that, and mysterious, so mysterious I cannot reconstitute them even as I try, because they are *people*, they walk on this earth, and they will die here.

As Frances Burnett wrote, there are only a few times in life when we think we are going to live forever. And I think one of them is when we are with our friends, laughing, eating, looking each other in the eye. I would rather write about friends than relations. Relations— parents, children, siblings, spouses—exist within a grid of social conceptions and expectations that have evolved over centuries, and though we may fail in these relations, though we may let the preconceived down, nowhere in these relations do I find the sheer unexpected *variety* that friendship offers, for no two friendships are based on the same thing, the bond between two friends has no explanation other than itself.

I have a friend who has never read a single word I have ever written. I love being with her.

I have a friend who is not a person I could ever be, even if I tried, nor would I want to be, and I love being with her.

I had a friend who peeled an orange in public for the first time when she was seventeen. I do not remember the first time I peeled an orange, but it was probably in front of another. Do any of us remember such an act, such a little act lost in so many other acts performed for the first time when we are children? My friend's mother was cultivated to the point of exoticism, and at the same time conservative and strict; at least that is how I remember her. She taught her daughter that to peel an orange, or any other fruit, in the presence of another person was perverse; you might as well undress in front of them. Fruit was peeled in the kitchen by servants and served naked on a plate with a little knife to the side. The logic of this is itself perverse—do not undress in public but appear there naked—and as a result of such logic my friend was apprehensive when I unpacked our lunch one sunny afternoon, spreading a blue napkin on the stone steps of a cathedral; we were two teenagers having an outing in the city, an adventure, and I had thought to bring a picnic. Hence two unpeeled oranges appeared on the napkin and I watched my friend's face change color as she told me the rules regarding oranges. I insisted that people did it all the time, no one would notice, not a head would turn if she ventured to try. Never before or since have I seen someone peel an orange with such exquisite delicacy. She took off the skin as if it were covered with tiny mother-of-pearl buttons, and her hands trembled every time a piece of skin came off and fell away like a little continent set adrift, revealing the flesh inside, which was sometimes translucent and bright and bursting with moisture, and at other times covered by a thin white cottony undergarment. And that was that, we ate our oranges in public as carelessly as any two girls, none of the passersby noticed anything historical, and years later when I ran into my old friend, and recalled that afternoon in the sun, she told me she hated oranges and never ate them, her mother was dead, and she had no memory of any picnic on the steps of a church.

I had a friend who loved apple trees and apple blossoms and apple orchards, he loved swimming in ponds and lakes, and making currant jam and jam from mulberries and playing the harmonica, but when he read, for he loved books, he read heavy German tomes. He was diagnosed with cancer and the treatment for his cancer caused a stroke that led to blindness, he was blind at the end, and I took him swimming in a lake, I held his hand and helped him wade out until the water was waist-high, and then I said that I would be his beacon, I would not move. And he swam, not far, not much, but he went under and came up utterly refreshed, and all the while I stood there with my arms outstretched and thought *look at me, look at me, I am helping a blind man swim*. And when my friend died, I actually felt *lucky* because my last words to him were *I love you*, and his last words to me were *I love you* and I thought that it didn't get any luckier than that, though of course it could have been luckier: he could have lived with his sight for the last few years of his life, he could have seen his apple trees and gone swimming without my help.

I had a friend in high school, I had a crush on him, he was gay but I didn't know it. I had other friends who were gay and my favorite teachers were gay but I didn't know it, and there were other teachers who were not gay and not my favorite who were having sex with students who were not my friends but I didn't know it, I found out years later, my friend told me all about it, and I was shocked. We were in our thirties then, and he was dying of AIDS. I mean, he had AIDS and knew he would probably die but was not certain; he didn't want to die but he did come to see me, twice, in what turned out to be the last year of his life. We sat in a diner in the middle of Michigan and he told me all this stuff that was going on in high school that I had been completely unaware of. None of the gay guys in high school had come out, and he talked about that, about how he knew I had a crush on him but he couldn't bring himself to tell me he was gay. We actually laughed about it, we were in our thirties and considered ourselves grown-ups, adults. Later I found out that I was not grown-up at thirty, but he never found out, he died before he could find out he wasn't a grown-up. Sitting in the diner I said to him *I am so sorry.* And he said *why, because I am gay?* I said *no, not that; because you are going to die.* And he said *I don't want to die, but, you know, these things happen.* These things happen—I think in that moment I must have grown up, but later I lapsed into childhood again, and it was another thirty years before I remembered his words—*these things happen*—and by then I had lost countless friends and family members, by then his words seemed the simplest statement of the truth I had ever heard. After the diner he wanted to take a strenuous hike through the dunes of Lake Michigan, he had had chemo and was weak but was determined to try this one thing while he still had the chance. He barely made it, we would stop every few yards so he could rest, but he would not give up or turn back, and when we reached the shore of the lake he opened his fly and pissed right into the water, I saw his penis for the first time, he had a huge grin on his face and he took off his baseball cap—he was bald beneath it—and waved it in the air like he was riding a bronco in a rodeo. His lover was at the opera when he died, and his mother called me to tell me her son was gone. I had never met her, and she said to me *he talked about you a lot in high school, and at the end—but I never understood—*

what was the nature of your relationship? I could tell this was awkward for her, that in her grief she wanted to know everything she could about her son's life and wondered whether he had had sexual relations with women as well as men. I told her the truth, I said *your son was my friend, we were always friends, he was a friend of mine, and I was very lucky.*

I have a friend who believes that birds have souls but humans do not. Although this may sound like the belief of a misanthrope, my friend is anything but that, she is unfaltering in her cheerfulness and kindness, she plays Ping-Pong and badminton with relish, and though she has suffered the blows and disappointments of life like the rest of us, they have never laid a mantle on her shoulders, and I have often wondered if her explication of souls is connected to her sense of contentment, if it is the secret key to a disposition we could all use. I have known her for most of my life, and she remains a mystery. Birds! Little brown birds!

I had a friend in high school with whom I felt a deep bond; we were both interested in religion and philosophy. In college she went the way of the Greek classics and, by a turn in the road, became a Buddhist. I went the way of English literature and, by a turn in the road, became a poet with a Zen approach to writing who used the word *God* in every third poem. When we were teenagers, we shared the belief that we were human beings on a spiritual journey, but by the time we were fifty we both pretty much knew we were spiritual beings on a human journey, and we expressed this belief by exchanging Christmas cards every December. We didn't see each other in all that time, and then one year I happened to be teaching near her and we managed to spend a day together. We were both divorced and living alone by then, and of course we had lunch in a nifty restaurant (she was a vegetarian, I was not) but the rest of the afternoon we spent in the old swimming pool behind my crumbling apartment complex (the Eden Roc, pink stucco, or what was left of it). And what did we do in the swimming pool? Not swim. We stood waist-deep in the water and saved the lives of hundreds of drowning wasps, picking them one by one out of the water while we lazily talked, without either of us mentioning the wasps and what we were doing for them; for three hours we stood there and had a rhythm going, wasp up wasp out, and I can't remember any of our chat, I only remember the wasps in a pile on the side of the pool, coming to realize in their squirming that they were still alive, though most of them crawled right back into the pool and we saved their lives twice. It was lovely to see my old friend again, but that afternoon we didn't quite act like human friends, we acted like reincarnated lotus buds who, if they wanted to float, had to clear their pond of debris, which amounted to a good deed.

When I was an adolescent behaving in irresponsible ways, I had two friends I adored: they were twins, a boy and a girl, their names began with the same letter and almost rhymed. He was feminine and she was masculine, he was lithe and delicate with a high voice while she was muscular with a low, gravelly voice. I was closer to her than to him, but as they were as close as close and always together it hardly made a difference. They were in a band; he played guitar and she played drums. I was not in the band but on Friday nights there was always a party in the basement of the twins' house and the band played, or practiced, which was basically the same thing. When they weren't playing we did things that we thought were outrageously funny, such as throwing breakfast cereal into the toilet bowl and pretending it was vomit. We went to my friends' house because their mother was a widow and every Friday night she went on a date, leaving the house to us. We would party, and though I no longer remember what that feels like, I know it involves a desperate need to forget something. At around midnight their mother would come home so drunk she had to be put to bed by her children, and often I would help them get her up on the bed and out of her shoes. We didn't think anything of it, obviously she had partied while we were partying and that's what Friday nights were for. This went on for two years and then my family moved away and I had new friends and went to a new school. But judging from the journals I kept then, my sole purpose in life was to find a way to get back to my old friends. Reading the journals it is quite clear I was in love, though I have no memory of feeling this way. We wrote letters for a few years, but by the time I graduated from high school we had lost touch altogether. Years later—I was in my fifties—I came across a box of their baby pictures and pictures of their early childhood. It seemed to me I had so many pictures of them that they must have none, and I wanted to return the pictures but hadn't a clue as to where the twins lived. Somewhere in Texas, I thought. I called information in Dallas, I called information in Houston, and then I gave up. The pictures meant nothing to me, they just took up space, so I threw them all out. And then about a year later my phone rang and it was her. She had found me. We talked for about thirty minutes—military, disability, cabin in the woods, dogs, mother had gotten sober and married a great guy but was dead now—and promised to stay in touch. I knew what would happen next: the phone rang and it was her brother, she had called him immediately after talking to me. So I chatted with him—military, commercial pilot, never married—and said goodbye. I didn't mention the pictures. The next day I got another call from his sister, inviting me to their high school reunion; I reminded her that I didn't go to high school with them, it had been junior high, but she said it didn't matter because she and her brother organized the reunion every year and could invite anyone they wanted and I wouldn't regret it because it was a blast, they rented a Ramada Inn in Dallas and partied for two days, a whole weekend, it was *the* event of the year, they lived for it, everyone lived for it, I would love it, it was a *blast*. I told her I didn't go to my own high school reunion, that I was not the "reunion type," that I was very busy anyway and didn't like to travel. She would not take no for an answer and called week after week begging me to come party in Texas. Finally I stopped answering the phone. She kept calling, I didn't pick up, and finally she stopped. I think she understood I was somehow not the same, I was not the same as I was at thirteen and I was not the same as they were now. I felt bad about the pictures, though; I don't really know how I came to have them, it must have been we were partying and the family album came out and either I stole them (because I was in love) or they were wantonly given away. But in the photographs my friends were so innocent, little children on tricycles or holding Easter baskets, and it saddened me to think of them as adults, having a blast in the Ramada Inn once a year; it fairly broke my heart, but then again I was just as sad over myself— look who I had become, having destroyed without thinking the childhood memories of another, just sitting there at my desk ripping the photos up, tossing them into the basket beneath me.

I have a friend whom I have never met; I am pretty sure we will meet next year because two of the friends I've written about here have died since writing this.

I have a friend I met once and only briefly and we have corresponded ever since. In the beginning, we wrote long letters using words, but for some years now we have not; now we exchange, by mail, flowering branches, birds' nests, tiny gloves, feather hats, and once she sent me the entire sweepings from her porch—shards of blue clapboard paint mixed with dirt, leaves, and debris: beauty by accident, as so many friendships are.

I have a friend who wishes she were not a human animal but an animal with fur. A fox, a dog, or a rabbit. This disturbs me so much I love her even more.

I have a friend I have known for fifty years. She is the purest poet I know, but she has not written a poem since she was twenty; instead she has chosen, day after day, to wear only blue or gray, and I consider this an ingenious, even perfect, solution to the problem of poetry and time.

I had a friend I loved for twenty-five years, and then the earth opened between us, and now we have not spoken in twenty-five years. But nearly every week I dream of her, so there is this sense, for me at least, that we still know and love each other, but only late in the night, behind closed eyes.

I have a friend who did "exactly the opposite of what one would have expected from the first" (as Proust says in a letter) and when this was done, my last beliefs in the architecture of reason and coherence were completely demolished, and as for the inevitable debris found among the ruins, I blew that away myself, though not as easily as one dispels a bit of dust. Thus I have a friend I love but do not trust and never will.

I had a friend who was only briefly my friend, he was the friend of a friend and I knew him for only two months while I was working on the West Coast, but one afternoon he performed an act of kindness that has flowered in me for half a century. When picking me up from work, merely giving me a ride home, he stood across the street with a brown paper bag in his hand, and in the bag was a muffin he had bought for me, no more than that, and yet at nineteen it was the greatest act anyone had ever performed in front of me—a muffin in a bag for a girl too sad and too young to say she was sad, to tell anyone, yet here he was, my friend, lifting and waving the bag from across the street. How do you thank someone for something like that? You don't, half a century passes, and even if you did they would think you were a lunatic, but you are not a lunatic because someone once gave you a muffin in a brown bag, assuring you that you were sane, and would be, forever.

I had a friend who, at a very sad time in my life, was more or less my only friend, and she was sad, too, and she was a dog. She was not my dog, I had never had a dog, I knew nothing about dogs, I had heard they were "man's best friend" but thought that was sentimental and without weight. My friend belonged to a very young couple— too young to be a couple, in my opinion—who lived in the apartment below mine. They fought all the time, especially at night. They screamed and hollered at each other and sounded a lot like an old married couple who fought, which is why I thought they were way too young to live like that. My friend, the dog, used to visit me when her parents (masters, owners?) fought; I would hear her scratching at my door, she couldn't bark because her vocal cords had been removed by her original owner (parent, master?). Her hips had been damaged in an accident and she wore a brace around her hind. I could hear her scratching at my door with her front paw and I would let her in, together we would sit and listen to the fighting coming up through the floor, she would be trembling and I would put my arms around her and we would stay like that for the longest time. I always had food and water for her, she knew right where they were on the floor, and since at that time I myself was eating very little on account of my sadness, I would eat a little something from my cupboard when she ate. So we would eat together and hold each other, and then her master (parent, owner?) would holler for her to come down and she would go, I would hold the door open for her and she would turn one last time to look at me before she limped down the stairs. She could not bark or whimper or make the least sound. I loved her. One day I put a silly cardboard frame over her head so that it sat on her neck and framed her face and I took her picture. The whole thing lasted no more than a minute, and today, thirty years later, her portrait still sits by my desk. I know she is dead but I don't know how the last years of her life turned out—one night the couple had an explosive fight, my friend came upstairs to sit with me, and in the morning her mother (owner, master?) packed the car and left, taking my friend with her. As I stood in the parking lot I could not bring myself to say goodbye, I didn't hug her or pet her, I just looked at her and walked inside. If she had anything to say she couldn't say it, nor could I. But I could cry and that was a blessing. Now when I think of dogs I understand that the relationship *is* very sentimental, and carries great and lasting weight, like any friendship.

I have a friend, and for several years we were both lost at the same time, at loose ends, adrift. He lived on the West Coast and I lived on the East Coast, and many nights we talked for hours on the phone, keeping each other company. Even the long silences were comfortable between us, but some of the things we said to each other were so strange I began writing them down, writing things down was everything to me and it was everything to him, someone who knew us well said we could complete each other's sentences, and that was true too. He would say "I can't talk to people who don't know what they are doing" when it was clear neither of us knew what we were doing. Once he said "I'm so slow," and I said "I know, you have a head of butter and a body of water," which he pretty much does, and another time he said "L. is so much smarter than I am ... no, not smarter but ... he has a wife." Then we would crack up and the minutes flew. Suddenly he would exclaim "Look at this, a helicopter! What would Kafka say?" He was always reporting on things happening outside his window—once he saw a mountain lion—while out my window I saw only squirrels. A dear friend of his died, and his wistful comment was "I am completely unable to make myself stutter." He was that smooth, butter and water. Then he lost another friend, suddenly and unexpectedly, and he said "No one knows what to say. That's why poetry exists." I was contemplating getting an aquarium, a large one, and his reaction was "You have to have a sense of irony to buy a gigantic aquarium in the first place, but once you start sitting in front of it and staring you've lost your sense of irony." We would always talk about what we were having, or just had, for dinner. I'd say "I just ate a plump little hand-fed hand-raised chicken, isn't that sad?" and he'd respond "I don't want to upset you because

you've already upset yourself, but all I ate today was cardboard."
Another conversation went like this: "Sorry, I'm just me these days";
"That's your problem, you're just you so snap out of it!" I would hear
his doorbell ring in the background and he would say "That's my dry
cleaning being delivered." To me that was insanely indulgent, but he
would remind me that his family were immigrants and say "We didn't
come to this country to change lightbulbs," then I'd remind him that
they came to this country because we *have* lightbulbs. It was just
banter, completely idle, and we loved it. We could say anything to
each other, and that is one of the great gifts of friendship. We shared
a wavelength, and we still do, though our lives are no longer adrift
and we don't talk nearly so often, but the sound of his voice is as
familiar to me as air. We often spoke out of the blue, without any
context, and once he said something totally unexpected, he said
"Women are incredible. I just wanted to say that, in case any women
are listening."

I have a friend who is the best-read human being I have ever known;
not only has he read everything you have ever heard of, read, or
hoped to read, he has read novels like *The Mysteries of Udolpho* and
Penguin Island, he has read *Lorna Doone*, he has read *The Exegesis
of Philip K. Dick*, he has read Duns Scotus, his idol is David Hume,
and although he is completely indifferent towards Shakespeare, my
friend is also the sanest person I know. Eccentric and sane, a dy-
namo combination. He has a beautiful, compassionate wife whom he
adores, two beautiful grown children whom he adores, and he lives

in a modest home that is one of the warmest and most welcoming I have ever been in. Yet his special place is in its basement, where he has a grotto, his refuge, his private sanctuary. This room is cold and damp and covered floor to ceiling with shelves holding his collections, which include a hundred porcelain figurines on whose faces unusual expressions have been caught, framed photographs of forgotten movie stars, a hundred peculiar ashtrays, a thousand tiny matchbooks, and everything in between. It resembles an antique store of the particular kind that a fetish-minded customer would buy out on the spot. A foreign director once wanted to film it, but my friend declined. This is where he keeps his books, and his postcards —of which he has over twenty thousand—arranged in metal filing cabinets. In middle age he suffered the proverbial collapse, after which he became a serious student of Buddhism, meditating daily in his grotto. He was born a Jew, the son of Holocaust survivors who so traumatized his development that their level of control and his level of guilt constantly collided—his mother would not allow him to wear worn, frayed jeans in high school because she didn't survive for her son to wear rags—and eventually he became not a misanthrope but a slightly misanthropic man, having learned early on through books and life that inhumanity is an ongoing reality. If "history teaches, but it has no pupils" (Gramsci), my friend is sitting in that otherwise empty classroom. Yet over the years his wife and family, his music, his dog, have brought him such genuine solace and love that he considers himself a fortunate man. One day I said to him his whole philosophy could be summed up in a sentence, *Life is ter-*

rible, terrible, and I am a fortunate man. He laughed with acknowl-
edgment. But sometime later it dawned on me that my friend, who
had spent his whole life escaping the clutch of his parents, had finally
come to a summation that was in effect theirs, for they had drummed
into him since he first gasped for air that life was terrible and he was
fortunate. Which is my philosophy entirely, for life *is* terrible, and I
am fortunate, fortunate to have such a friend, who keeps me ever
aware and in check, as on the day he said to me from out of the blue
*oh, are you so cozy in your life you can turn down a red-flocked bear
ashtray?*

I have a friend who died, yet every time I think of him I smile, and
am never sad. How can you not smile when you recall a man who,
given the choice, would only eat white food? His favorite meal, which
he often served to guests, was boiled spaghetti with cheese sprin-
kled on top, cheese you shook from a can, and for dessert a boxed
Boston cream pie with the chocolate glaze diligently scraped off. A
man who was such a romantic his idea of a pickup line was "You
have all the colors of October in your hair, come and have a doughnut
in my car." He also dumped a bucket of sand on the floor of his car
so he could "take the beach with him" wherever he went. A masterful
writer who had published to acclaim but fell out with the times and
in his dotage announced with glee that a few paragraphs were ap-
pearing in *Yankee* magazine. Someone who recited Shelley and Keats
in the middle of a conversation about pudding. A man who was de-
termined to tap a maple tree for syrup, and upon tapping the lone

spindly tree in his front yard announced with pride that a cup of sap had produced a teaspoon of syrup that he gave as a gift to his neighbor's dog. The last time I saw my friend was the night of a full moon when he desired us to view it from the end of a pier so dangerously dilapidated it had been cordoned off by a chain and an ordinance. He drove to the chain, got out of his car, unhitched the chain, and drove us to the end of the pier where we sat in silence as the moon rose over the ocean. Finally he turned to me and said *they can't keep the moon out.*

I have a friend I have known since the day she was born. She is not my daughter, or my sister, but the daughter of a friend, at least she was the daughter of my friend for the first twenty years of her life before she became a *friend*, my friend. This came as a surprise to me, I had never considered that someone you knew before she could feed herself would one day be having dinner with you, holding a fork. If we are at the movies and go to the ladies' room together I don't think of her as being in diapers, though she once was and I knew her then. It is a mysterious thing how one person becomes another, and I cherish her friendship as utterly distinct from any others I have. But because she is thirty-five years younger than I am, and in all probability I will die before she reaches her full adulthood—before she is my age—I sometimes feel like a wild duck flying over her head, knowing all the time we have spent together will one day be no more than an occasional vivid memory for her (unlike a parent, whom one thinks of constantly). And then I realize that this is true of all friendships—they are wild ducks flying overhead—and that my friendship with her is no different than any other, and therefore perfect.

I had a friend I had known for years but we never lived in the same place at the same time, and then we did. For six months we lived in the same city and had dinner every week on the same night in the same restaurant at the same time at the same table and ordered the same thing (wild mushrooms in cream sauce) and drank the same wine (Sancerre). During dinner he told me the story of his life in increments, dinner by dinner, like a serialized novel. They were wonderful dinners and because we were moving from his birth to the present, and because the story of a heterosexual stockbroker who becomes a bisexual surrealist poet is a long one, we were always the last to leave the restaurant, the staff came to know us and let us linger at our table while they prepared to close for the night. My friend and I were doing the same work but because he was paid twice what I was he insisted on paying and would never let me pick up the bill. He did agree that I could pay for our last dinner and that on that occasion we would go somewhere new. Because I wanted to repay him in any way I could I chose an even more expensive restaurant, a Japanese one that was written up in all the papers. It was terrible. The food was so minimal we would look at our plates and make up ridiculous haiku on the spot, staring at a shred of vegetable floating in water. There were a hundred kinds of sake and we tried a great many of them, giving them titles. Haunted Bell. Chrysanthemum Tragedy. Nightingale Hit by a Fan. As the night wore on the names grew increasingly Western and literary until we were drinking Forlorn Incubus, and Apropos of Wet Snow. Shared misery can be a joy. I saw my friend once more before he died—we had dinner in a foreign country—and we spent that dinner talking about all our other dinners. Dinner with friends, it doesn't get any better than that. When you eat dinner with friends, the ones you really love and no other, you have reached a pinnacle you don't see, but it is there. Look around the table—"*in the still garden the meal shines for a gathering of friends*"— and if someone starts clearing it, put your hand on their arm ever so lightly, ever so briefly, pause that plate in midair.

I had a friend when I was ten, and she was a Mormon. We played together after school and on the weekends, and one night her mother invited me to stay for dinner. It was a large family, and they sat at a round table, and when it was time to say grace each one of them folded their arms in front of their chest, which startled me, as that was something my mother did when she was angry, when she stood in the kitchen and let you know. We said grace in my family, but we folded our hands together and bowed our heads, and no one could ever tell who was angry and who was not. When I ate with my friend's family, I thought they were all angry with God, and it confused me. Why would you pray when you were angry with God? I was too polite to ask my friend why Mormons did this, so for a long time it stewed in me. I had another friend at that time who was also Mormon, and one day she took me to her basement and showed me what her family kept down there—huge burlap sacks of lentils and beans and rice.

She said this was the food her family would live on when there was an apocalypse. I asked her what an apocalypse was and she said it was an event that would cause the whole planet to explode and burn. I did not understand why anyone would want to survive such a thing but was too polite to say so. Then I remembered the Mormons were angry when they prayed, and why not, they had to survive in ashes and live on beans. Suddenly I understood and things began to make sense to me, at the age of ten, thanks to my friends.

I had a friend in high school who was not my best friend but she lived closest to me in the city and it was easy to walk to her house on the weekends. She lived in a house and I lived in an apartment. Her family was sophisticated in ways that were new and mysterious to me. Her father, I found out years later, was a CIA agent whose cover was working as a cultural attaché with an emphasis in Asian art. These were the "days of Vietnam," as we refer to them now, which sounds so peculiar in retrospect, as if a fad for straw or silk had swept through the country. My friend's mother came from a wealthy Southern family and had once been a professional ballerina, a fact that deeply impressed me, as even my English teacher (and I excelled in English) told me I was a *klutz* without a single bodily grace belonging to any of the nine muses. He had been watching me through a classroom window as I tried, on the court below, to hit a tennis ball. Later he went so far as to insult my clothing, telling me to my face my dress was ridiculous, and so it was, a brown shift with huge turquoise polka dots, a Peter Pan collar and a big floppy bow. My sister had made it, she made all my clothes. We weren't allowed to wear pants to school. My friend's sister took fencing lessons in a white bodysuit; she had a *saber* and a *grilled mask*. It was all too much. My friend had several fur coats that were so odd and interesting you couldn't guess what animal they were made from. I joked once that she was wearing her monkey coat. It occurs to me now that it probably *was* a monkey coat, as monkeys can be found in all the Asian countries her father, supposedly collecting the antique heads of Buddha, traveled to. So that was the situation. My mother adored my friend, she liked my friend better than any of my other friends because when meeting my mother for the first time my friend had *curtsied*. I think my mother had waited her whole life for that moment. My mother loved fruit. I think she would as soon have married a pear as my father. There was always a big bowl of fruit in the kitchen. Liver-spotted bananas, and green grapes as translucent as jade, though if I ate the grapes, the arthritic stems that remained terrified me, I imagined them as crippled hands coming to get me. And there were always apples, her favorite. In those days there weren't *kinds* of apples, you couldn't say "I feel like a Gala," or "Pick up some Granny Smiths," there were only, well, apples. They were red, all shaped the same, and perfectly tasteless. My mother kept another bowl of fruit in the dining room, and all of that fruit was artificial. When I was younger it was plastic but by the time I was in high school it had all turned to bone china. In my mother's mind, there was a very big difference between a plastic orange and an orange made from china, and if you couldn't tell the difference you had no taste, none at all. It was the difference between a handshake and a curtsy. Years and years later, I wrote a poem and in the poem are the passing words *a world where no one ever even curtsies anymore*. And I have noticed through the years that many readers want, even demand, a backstory to anything that is ever written, and now I have given them *the entire backstory* of these fleeting words, and I feel for a moment like my friend, who curtsied in front of my mother, something my mother had always wanted, and got once.

When I walk through a city I see many strange faces, and though none leave a trace I know they have friends. Who are their friends, whose friends are they? For wherever I walk, images of my friends go with me.

I have a friend who used to be a dancer. She once choreographed and performed a dance I have never forgotten. She danced to Al Green singing "How Can You Mend a Broken Heart." She was solo on the stage, and a spotlight followed her as she moved. She was wearing a paper bodysuit, and as she moved the paper tore, at first in tiny slits at the seams, and then in big gashes, rip after rip until she was dancing in shreds, practically naked. It was so bold and beautiful and sad, and happened once and once only; it was something to behold, and then it vanished from the earth.

LETTER TO ELIZABETH BISHOP

Dear Elizabeth,

Margot, whom you have never met, says that my outfit is one you would not be caught dead in, but as you *are* dead, I am of the surest that you would be happy to be seen alive in it, if you could. I am writing you from Saratoga Springs, New York and it is not even the coldest spring but the worst February, the light is not strong enough to walk across the room. We are here celebrating your life and letters and I suppose the poems are the most of it but they celebrate themselves and I am not here to say anything about that, however I know you will be interested in the things that have changed, poetry not being among them, but when one is of a certain age and has thought all night about death, one eventually realizes that one wants not to die not because of never seeing one's beloveds again—shameful as that is—but because one wonders what the cars will look like, what assassinations will happen and where and when, how all manner of things in and of themselves will change, the shape of objects, newer and newer food, and shoes and hats and such, all the stuff of the world, the thingness. For instance there is a substance called velcro, a kind of cloth with the raised texture of a baby porcupine, one whose quills have not quite hardened, and two pieces of this cloth, when held together, create a bond, eliminating the need for zippers, buttons, laces, and ties. One would think we had an abiding human need for and interest in buttons and laces but apparently not, things go the way of things the way the flesh goes the way of flesh. Oh Elizabeth I am sorry to say we are also now living in the End of the Age of Paper, another substance that is fast afloat downstream in the direction of some final extinction. This will be hard for you to believe, yet remember the letter you once wrote (not to me; your letters, you will be aghast to hear, have gone and gotten themselves published, I don't know whom to blame)—well, in one letter you said, writing from Brazil to Boston, that if you did not own a Black Watch plaid wool blazer you would positively *die*, and you sent a little picture of one in the letter and asked them to send you one right away, enclosing, presumably, enough money to cover the cost of the blazer and its postage to the southern hemisphere: well, I saw two days ago, in a jumble heap of woolens at the thrift store, Charity Shop to you, a very long woolen scarf—at least three feet long—of Black Watch plaid, made in Scotland, the match to your jacket. And I did not buy it, though I toyed with the idea in your honor, no, Elizabeth, I left it there in the dirty heap. Why? Because the Age of the Black Watch Plaid has passed, no one wears it anymore, you would not be caught dead in it, even if you were alive. It is as charming as ever, that plaid, but its existence harks back to the time before women alive today existed. Why does it still exist, you may ask, and it exists precisely because it is useless, like all beautiful things Elizabeth, your poems and jacket among them, they persist in their secret obscurity, they go on and on wearing the shoes of a ghost who

THE GABLES

We came to The Gables for the first night of our engagement. I told my fiancé this is *exactly* what I want our bedroom to look like! I have never seen a headboard that thrilled me so. Pillows with chocolate on them, flowers in the fireplace, towels folded in the shape of swans—and a journal next to the bed, so I can tell him how I feel! As I lie here on this magnificent bed I surely know this is how Empress Alexandra felt in her mauve boudoir—of course she was married to the Czar of Russia but I know this is the relaxing luxury she received—plus I was in Vermont! "We shall return," as the General said, how could we not?

I think it was all part of God's plan—to give us a warm bath with many bubbles. To make us a King & Queen. So while the usual haste of romantic passion was spent slumbering, our stay could not have been more peaceful. We were King & Queen filled with attention to detail. Thank you.

(The Gables was the first place my Lady stayed in the United States and I know she will always remember it. The adjectives could fill a book. I'm sure no one ever came close to our first experience. It was

one of the most beautiful October nights I have ever seen, here in our
beautiful room. Merci!)

This is the first time my husband and I have spent the night away from our infant son. It was wonderful! It was so quiet here, at one point we went outside just to hear some background noise.

It is my job to be professionally spoiled. We are back for the third time.

Heaven in an ice bucket!

The Lord told us to come here and gave my husband many dreams and confirmations about The Gables. What place other than a castle would the King have his children stay? This weekend is simply a celebration of the ménage à trois of us three: the Lord, my husband, and me.

Forever will I remember this night into the days of longevity.

11:45, only 15 minutes left in the greatest day of my life.

The Gables is an inspiration that creates a new illusion of life! Thank you for that.

The atmosphere here demands relaxation.

It was so nice not having to worry about anything except what we were going to do next!

The Gables is so beautiful that I have always had a great appreciation for architecture. I would love to stay here again, but our next special occasion will most likely be in Belgium, Japan, or even England.

AFFORDABLE VACATION

Pretend you are a penny, travel as one for two weeks, come home and tell your friends where you have been, where you stayed, what you saw, the people you met and all your adventures. You might not have any pictures, but you came home spent and anyone will be able to see it was a wild vacation, one that makes two weeks in an Italian villa seem boring, yep, everyone agrees you are lucky, your face is shining and you're ready to leave again at a moment's notice.

AN AMERICAN HAIKU

The days were long and the nights even longer. It had been a long time since the last haiku and the haikuist did not know where the next seventeen syllables would come from. When they came they would come unexpectedly, arrive unannounced, he knew that much from his years of experience, yet years of experience counted for very little when it came to haiku. Returning from a recent trip, the smell of Cinnabons in an airport held out the promise of a haiku, but it didn't seem very haikuish in the end. After he boarded his connecting flight he wondered if the suddenly vanishing smell wasn't perhaps more haikuish than the first whiff, but a haiku should not be a memory, it should be endlessly occurring, and so he further nixed the sound of the car wheels rumbling over the highway when, as a child, he had slept on the floor in the back of his family's car, his face so close to the road—separated, really, by only an inch or two of metal—that the sound of the powerful motion beneath him seemed to him, a mere five-year-old, to be the heartbeat of another world, a world he could not quite enter, though he be inches from it. After the haikuist returned from his journey, the only memorable part being the smell of Cinnabons baking in the airport, he resumed his daily life, shopping for food at the supermarket where, on a flagpole, a gigantic American flag was rippling in slow motion over the parking lot, moved by the March wind, backlit almost to transparency by the March light, and this sight struck him as suitable for a haiku, but no sooner had he parked than the idea vanished. Coming home he drove past the local thrift store, where in the window hung a very old wedding dress next to an old blue suitcase, and he almost stopped, thinking he had found his haiku, or it had found him, but he drove on home. At home he made an important phone call to a government agency and was put on hold for forty-two minutes while the agency played Muzak full of static. He sat mindlessly eating chips from a bag which crumbled and crunched as he emptied it, as if the bag itself were one big chip, and these forty-two minutes on hold he mentally tried to reduce to seventeen syllables (including the chips) but when his patience paid off and an actual government agent addressed him, he forgot all about his haiku. His conversation with the agent was frustrating, and afterwards, to relieve his stress, he drove to the local swimming pool. Submerged in the lap lane, every time he turned his head underwater he had a view of the legs of the weak and elderly in the therapy lane, all sizes and shapes of legs were slowly pumping underwater, and the haikuist was so moved by the sight he was determined to write a haiku capturing the moment, but then he felt guilty, using the weak and elderly as inspiration. He argued with himself for a while, got out of the pool, showered, dressed, and drove home. On the way there he saw a man sitting on the curb at a neighborhood grocery store, the man's head was bent over a lotto card and he was scratching at it with a coin. It almost looked like he was writing, and the haikuist was reminded of himself—when would *he* get lucky and write his next haiku? It had been more than a month. A month filled with many haikuish moments, to the extent he was beginning to think of one long haiku, rising and subsiding like waves in the ocean, coming forward and dropping a seashell, which, whenever the haikuist picked it up, he put to his ear and heard again the long road rolling away beneath him when as a child he slept on the floor of his parent's car. Then the sea took the shell back.

TEETH OF NOON

When I was nineteen I enrolled in a college in the Swiss Alps. It had once been a sanatorium such as Thomas Mann describes in *The Magic Mountain*. Every dorm room had a balcony overlooking the Dents du Midi, the Teeth of Noon, seven jagged snow-covered peaks. Nabokov lived down the mountain in a hotel on a lake with swans. Nearer than that was the Château de Chillon, where Byron and Shelley stopped one summer afternoon while sailing together. In the afternoon I'd sit on my balcony wrapped in a blanket, reading. Whenever I looked up, there were the Teeth of Noon sparkling at me. Down the hall was the old operating theater, larger than the average dorm room, so that six girls roomed there together. They were my friends and I spent a lot of time in the operating theater, just hanging out, lying on the bunks. One day a rumor flew there was going to be a drug raid that evening, I had half a pound of hashish hidden under my bed so I had no choice but to eat it all before the raid, which never happened. That same evening I was playing a hooker in a Sartre play and forgot all my lines. I just made stuff up, and thus ended that career. Down the road was an extraordinary pastry shop and an English bookstore, for the English had been coming to the village for a long time and enjoyed sweets and reading. And the local fire brigade needed to practice their drill on the sanatorium, which was ten stories high, so they asked for volunteers to go up on the roof and slide down a canvas shoot into the arms of a fireman. I was the first to volunteer and slid down the canvas shoot into the arms of a Swiss firefighter. Oh my life was dreary, my whole existence bored me, so I suddenly decided to drop out and left school without telling my parents or anyone else, except my psychology teacher, who came to my room and asked me did I want to talk to someone before I made such a rash decision. I said no, my mind was made up, it was strong and clear. I was young, I wanted so much more. Like Youth Itself I did not grasp I was living a dream of exhilarating newness. I walked away, I said goodbye to the Teeth of Noon and began my bewildered life.

THE EFFUSIVE

It's been a great year. I turned seventy and my brother shot himself.
I am a tall person who is small and mean inside. For instance, on
Christmas morning I wake and begin to pack away all my Christmas
decorations. I love Christmastime (December 1–24) but I hate the
glare of Christmas morning, the sound of crumpling wrapping paper,
and the belief that it is still actually Christmas. I like to get a head
start on things, which is why I am constantly planning for death. I
throw away birthday cards on the morning of my birthday. In seventy
years I have read a great many books but I do not remember—cannot
tell you—a single sentence or line from any of them. It seems to me
I am merely a walking trunk of titles. I would rather read a children's
book than cook. Yet I believe I am a genuine person, an ordinary, nor-
mal creature who loves flowers unless they are yellow, though wild
yellow tulips grow rampant in the woods next to my house and I like
them so much one year I picked a bunch only to discover they wither
instantly when picked. *Never hit a child or pick a wildflower* is ancient
wisdom, passed on for so long it has finally disappeared. I find this
sad, now that I have learned my lesson. I was beaten when I was a
child, but like Christmas morning so what to all that. Nothing stops
my life from moving forward towards my death. I hate chocolate (the

people who love me keep giving it to me, even if I put it in writing they will not stop). I hate parties of all kinds, and give two magnificent ones every year. One is at Christmas, and one is in the spring when the wild yellow tulips are in bloom. My guests and I, we sit in silence and stare at the tulips through the trees, it is a genuine moment of feeling sad that we can't pick them, knowing we should not, and understanding they will wither whether or not they are picked.

THE NOVEL

I was reading in front of the fire, it was a luxury, it was snowing out-side, bitterly cold, but there in my snuggling I was on fire with my book, a recently published novel that had been translated into over twenty languages, I was in the middle of a sentence when a thought of my own intruded—somewhere in the world someone else was reading the same novel and was in sync with my own reading, reading the same sentence I was, and I was gripped with this knowledge and with fear and terror—I had thought I was alone but someone else was reading with me, the same sentence, apace with me, word by word my terror spread, I wanted to be the only one reading, to be in the middle of *a solitary act*, that is why I had built the fire in the first place, why I had lain down on the couch in front of the fire, but I was not, unquestionably I was not the only one reading this book at this moment, and I was so utterly de-selved, so turned around and so tor-tured I stopped reading, I stood up and commanded myself to walk, I told myself that the other reader would be going on ahead, ahead and alone, we would no longer be synchronized and I could again be an individual with individual pursuits, I walked around the room with my pulse beating, my heart racing, I tried to calm myself, I said to myself *this is ridiculous*, and then I lay down again and began to read, safe in the knowledge that the other reader was at least a page ahead of me, what a relief, I did not have to share my moment-to-moment experience with him—or her—or they—in Tashkent or Paris, Granada or Stuttgart—and I kept reading, I was calm, I forgot about my irrational fears of a moment ago, and some hundred pages on, when they were entirely forgotten, the author began writing about the fear of the doppelgänger, the twin, the mirror, the echo, the identical other, and I was paralyzed again, not with fear of the other reader, who was by now pages and pages ahead of me, but with the new fear that the author inhabited me, and had my thoughts, and that my experience was no longer my own, and never had been.

THE BOOK

That book sat on my various shelves for decades until I got around to it, and then it seemed to be written especially for me. I hope this provides some hope to the other unread books surrounding me who are wondering what will happen to them when I die. I don't have the heart to tell them they will all be sold or recycled and will never see one another again. I think we do books an injustice by cramming them so closely together on shelves. A certain intimacy inevitably occurs and when they find themselves separated and stickered with a new price that underscores their loneliness, there is little that a new reader can do to ameliorate their sorrow but to read them and say *Old Friend, you were written especially for me.*

CHILLY OBSERVATION

Do you know the story of the woman who went to a taverna in Greece, her table was set on the beach, after a while the tide came in, the water covered her legs and the legs of the table and the waiter continued to serve her, going back and forth from the kitchen as if nothing were happening? People often wonder what it is like to be old, and a few actually ask.

THE PLUM AND THE DEVIL

This plum sat in the sun for three hours, its skin split apart and its syrup began to ooze out. When I bit into it I thought of William Carlos Williams, and I thought of Anne Frank, who had a can of sardines thrown to her over a barbed-wire fence but another prisoner caught it and ran away. And I thought of the three or four blank pages between her last diary writing and her unfinished novel, which she had begun by turning the account-book, the one she was currently using, upside down and writing forward from the back. I thought of things upside down, I thought of how Williams's plum was cold and mine was warm, the sun and the icebox. I thought of the blank pages separating the child from the writer. As if in a few years they would meet. I bit into the plum, it was the most delicious plum I had ever eaten, it was July ninth, 2022, and I thought of the line *How paltry is the Devil's power to destroy compared to what can momentarily be.* The plum, the plum! But what about the novel?

Notes

"Letter to Elizabeth Bishop": Some years ago I was asked to take part in an art show centered on Elizabeth Bishop; all I had to do was sit at a table and type, using an old black heavy typewriter. As she must have. It was a one-day event and I think the gallery was open about four hours. I remember I wore close-fitting slacks, a turtleneck sweater, and ballet flats, thinking I looked circa 1959. I typed several letters to friends to whom I owed a letter and then I was at a loss and decided to write Elizabeth. This piece, un-abridged, ends in the middle of a sentence because the gallery was closing and I was eager to stop, stand up, and go home.

"The Gables": Often when I travel I am lodged in a B and B, and often by the side of the bed there are blank journals where guests are welcome to write their impressions of the place; this piece is a compilation of some of those entries. I have made a few changes.

Acknowledgments

Some of these pieces have appeared in *The Arkansas International, FIELD-NOTES, The Glacier, Granta, Jung Journal, Mississippi Review, Passages North, The Poetry Review* (London), *The Sewanee Review,* and *Then Again: Vintage Photography Reimagined by One Artist and Thirty-One Writers.*

The epigraph by Francis Jammes is translated by Bruce Whiteman.

The opening of "Golden Crumbs" comes from English novelist Florence Warden (1857–1929).

The opening of "The Book" is taken verbatim from a letter my friend Lawrence Sutin wrote me.

The line in italics at the end of "The Plum and the Devil" is by Jack Gilbert.

What is it, the heart,
is it the sound of the pine trees
blowing in the painting?